WE Are the Magic
We **ARE** the Magic
We Are **THE** Magic
We Are the **MAGIC**

Also by Alishea Jurado

Growing Our Hearts: New Baby, New Groove
Children's Book, October 2023

One Little World: A Song for Peace
Children's Book, October 2024

We Are the Magic

Motherhood Poems

Alishea Jurado

JamTree Publishing
Miami, FL

Copyright © 2024 by Alishea Jurado. All rights reserved. No part of this book may be reproduced, stored in a retrievel system or transmitted in any form or by any means, electronic, mechanical, photocopy, recording, or otherwise, without written permission of the author and publisher, except in the case of brief quotations embodied in critical articles and reviews.

Library of Congress Control Number: 2024910894.
Paperback ISBN: 979-8-9889345-3-0

Book cover illustration by Marta Susic
Book cover design by Marta Susic and Melissa Regina
Interior design by Alishea Jurado and Melissa Regina
Editorial production by Kjersten Faseler

www.alisheajurado.com

To my aunts, Karen and Kitty,
I could write an entire book and still not capture
the depth of my gratitude and love for you.
There are no words to describe
your unwavering commitment to lifting and resuscitating
all who teeter on the brink of collapse.
Perhaps I'll need to find a new medium to convey it—
skywriting? Interpretive dance?
You name it!

To my mom, Michele,
I wish everyday to be more like you.
Thank you for being my teacher in how to truly love others
and for the gift you gave me to fully love myself.

Note to Reader

Our stories matter— they heal wounds, lift spirits, and remind us that we are not alone in this beautifully nuanced journey. I offer this collection of poems as a way to honor the lost and found of Motherhood that so many of us have experienced. I also want to celebrate the transformative and grounding power within our friendships, the roles we establish and reject within ourselves, and the ways in which sharing our stories illuminates a path toward wholeness.

May these verses help you recognize your own magic and remind you that in every challenge, every moment of joy, and every step toward healing, you are never alone. And if by some cosmic chance reading these poems inspires you to tell your stories, whether in writing or conversation, I hope you will share them with me, too.

Through the dark and light,
Alishea

@dr.alisheajurado
www.alisheajurado.com

Table of Contents

Note to Reader	VII
We ARE the Magic	2
Motherhood Lost	3
The Space We Hold	4
Motherhood Found	5
I Was Still a Mother in the Furiuos Wakings	6
Finding My Groove	7
My Mystery School Had Already Begun	8
Motherhood Transforms Me	9
Advice from My Friend's Mother	10
A Dream Is a Wish	11
Finally Understanding the Aerosmith Anthem	12
The Relics We Release	13
Apologies to the Sea	14
A Living Draft	15
This Is How We Roll	16
Text Thread With a Friend	17
That Friend	19
Sacred Surrender	20
Sacred Language	21
Pure Magic	23
Pure Gold	24
My Best Friend	25
Happy BIRTHday	26
A Seasoned Love	27
The Momentary Victor	29

30	Drunk on the Muse
31	Writing Is a Sacred Mother
32	The Forces at Play
33	Fear and Love and Love and Rage
35	When Boundaries Emerge
36	The Storms Without and Within
37	The Moon and Me
38	Resentment
39	The Era of Yin
41	My Mother's Gift
42	Exhale, And Release
43	I Am My Most Gracious Host
44	Nostalgia
45	Aha Moments
47	Motherhood Math
48	Too Beautiful to Capture
49	Transcendence Is an Altar, Too
50	Mothering in Community
51	I've Got a Mom for That
53	Witchy and Wise
54	The Collective Wisdom Is Strong
55	Rhythm and Pulse
56	Reclaiming Our Birthright
57	On Preparing for Motherhood
59	Stepping Into Our Power
62	Acknowledgements

We Are the Magic

When we say the magic flows *through* us—
we are wrong.

When we say we are the magic *makers*—
we are wrong.

When we envision magic surrounding us,
waiting to be conjured and created,
shaped and sharpened,
unfolded and unveiled,

we miss our magnificence.

Let me remind us, again and again,
dear sisters,
we are not the magic makers.

We ARE the magic.

All we have to do—

is be.

Motherhood Lost

We are body-burdened from this Motherhood pace—
from the absence of fluidity that aligns with our nature.

This perpetual state of edge and strain defines us—
our bodies a landscape of tension
from the more-than-ourselves we're asked to be.

This is our Motherhood lost.

The Space We Hold

We hold space for our children—
for their nuanced love.

A space to explore the sacred nature
of their imperfection.

Because we are body-bound,
this space we hold is made
by excavating pieces of our soul.

How do we create the infinite space needed
to hold and mother
and still fit the fullness of ourselves
in these body containers?

We must not be body-bound.

We must learn the art of soul expansion.

This is our Motherhood found.

Motherhood Found

The essence
    of our Motherhood found is—

sweet and smokey,
    like honey on fire,

feral and raw,
    like wild streaking,

bold and rebellious,
    like a Phoenix
        emerging from crystals.

I Was Still a Mother in the Furious Wakings

For many nights after coming home,
he woke often
and I woke furious,
forgetting I had a child,
until I realized he was crying.

I would shake my body into Motherhood,
scoop him up,
and we'd rock and carry on gently,
together, for whatever the night offered.

This furious waking continued for days, weeks,
possibly months—
it's hard to remember in the blur of it all.

What I do remember is the first night,
in our gentle carrying on,
realizing that I had awoken so tenderly,
so full of ache to hold him,
so full of awe,
forgetting my layers of exhaustion.

I remember thinking that I must now,
finally, be a mother—
desperately hoping this new nurture in my nature
would nestle in permanently.

Finding My Groove

With my second, I was a little less classical,
a little more jazz.

I was tuned in to the ephemeral nature
of ages and stages,
and that all would flow
in its time and place.

There was a surrender and release
to the reality that,
regardless of my perfectly scored plans,

my realm of control was actually,
comically,
quite limited.

So, instead, I was riffing to the rhythm of chaos,
creating structure within spontaneity,
taking creative risks with the
expression of my Motherhood,
and improvising my little heart out.

My Mystery School Had Already Begun

My second son was born to an already mother
who ebbed and flowed more often,

who knew all milestones would be met
at his own perfect pace,

who knew better than to define herself
by his doing,

who celebrated her friends' children
with no attention to a gap or gain of comparison,

who had already mastered the art of fevers,
and strep, and the horrid hand, foot, mouth
that takes the house by storm—

who didn't have to question when to intervene
with a body battling these ailments,

who understood the divine nature of our union—
that our journeys, though not the same,
are both parallel and intersecting all at once,

who allowed imperfection to drip and roll
down the curve of her back,

while celebrating her own milestones.

Motherhood Transforms Me

I've been a fierce mama bear,
fiery mama dragon,
watchful mama wolf,
graceful mama butterfly,
readied mama snake,
and quiet mama mouse.

I've been a vast mama ocean,
mysterious mama swamp,
frozen mama iceberg,
scorching mama desert,
wild mama jungle,
and majestic mama mountain.

It depends on the season
(and, likely, what someone has said
to my child).

Advice from My Friend's Mother

Just love them.

When it hurts, when it's hard,
when you've failed, when you've fallen,
when you're floating, when you're fearless,
when you're raging, when you're warring,
after worry, after wisdom,
through the wounds, and through the scars—
just love them.

And love yourself, too.

A Dream Is a Wish

My love for you is embodied
in this single wish—
that you experience the fullness
of a sensory life—

that your nose tracks the deep scent
of pure magic in others,
your ears interpret
the profound poetry of silence,
your feet feel the wind
pushing your resolve forward,
your eyes witness hope
boldly reaching through the dark,
and your tongue savors the exquisite blend
of raw hope and absolute grit,

that when your eyes close to sleep,
body wild-weary,
your soul swirls with the sweetest songs,
tracing the outline of your tender heart,
quieting your mind,
and wrapping you in the most vivid dreams.

Finally Understanding the Aerosmith Anthem

I could never fully relate to the lyrical musings
on staying awake to hear a lover breathe—

I never really longed to inventory a partner so wholly
to willingly barter my own rest
to soak up their sleeping splendor.

It wasn't until cradling a child overcome by sleep
that I found myself adoring every little part—
cheeks, eyelashes, puckered lips—
all of the elements that transform in the day
as their features and personality marry.

In the night, when personality fades
and features reign free,
regardless of the years that have passed,
I find myself overcome
by their perfectly peaceful beings,
and the acute awareness
that I don't want to miss a thing.

The Relics We Release

I notice it's happened again
when I see your pant hems
kiss your ankles.

I brace myself for the montage
of all you've done
in the era of these pants.

I wonder where they'll go
when they kiss your brother's ankles.

Apologies to the Sea

I'll return all else to the sea, but this—
moonbeams that held our wishes,
your small hand in mine,
the sunlit whirl of your water play,
the way anything shiny became your treasure,
your soft breath while sleeping,
your whimsical versions of familiar words,
the feel of your little body curled into mine,
the softness of your dimpled cheek against my thumb,
and every moment in between.

A Living Draft

I often wonder if my oldest, my little artist,
will also write poems.

And if he does, I wonder if he'll weave me through them.

And if he does, I wonder if the theme of my mothering
will pour out in lines of rivers and magic,
fire and rage, or some breed of both.

In a moment of weakness, while he puts on his pjs,
I decide not to wonder and ask,
if he were to write such a poem,
what he would say.

He stands to recite, as though it's the most natural thing—
body relaxed, deep breath in and begins.

I listen as he expounds upon
what I do, what I wear, what I say.

But the ending—
the ending is a magical profession of love,
absent of fire and rage,
and I am filled with rivers of relief.

I wrap myself around him and his sweet poem,
mentally reciting vows as my lips meet his hairline,
knowing this version is only a working draft.

This Is How We Roll

She told me that some days
I'd rock up to work—
outfit on point,
kids dropped off on time,
the imprint of joy
and lightness
across my laugh lines.

And I will have remembered
all the pump parts.

She said other days—
I'd call in late
and rush in
with the imprint of meltdowns
and tantrums
and marital arguments
across my brow.

And I will, undoubtedly, have milk stains
seeping through my shirt.

She said I'd never really know which
day would be which,
so best just learn to roll.

I've become a very smooth stone.

Text Thread with a Friend

Me:
"Not sure this resonates at all,
but it's the poem I'm working on
and I thought, after our chat today,
you might need it—
if not, we'll laugh!"

[sends poem]

Her:
"I feel that. Very much so.
The nuances of what I'm willing to lose
versus what I want to keep
and how to navigate it all.
I chose the "stay-at-home mom" life,
so that's a large part
of the conversation I'm always
having with myself."

Me:
"We choose a lot
before we can understand
the meaning behind the choices.
I feel like we can only know
in hindsight and likely,
we'd still choose the same path,
we'd just know what we're giving up
or what we'll need as far as support."

Her:
"And if we understood,
then we wouldn't have to
mourn the loss as much.
But I don't actually think you
could ever understand.
Like you said, hindsight."

Me:
"I love that—
the not mourning because we gave it up,
versus losing it without warning."

That Friend

I say, "I want to feel expansive—
maybe clear some space in the center of my chest,
just enough to feel the wind whisper
through my ribs."

I wait patiently for the bold blend
of wisdom and wit I've
come to adore all these years.

"Well," she says,
and my smile surprises me,
readied with anticipation,
"a bubble bath isn't going to do it."

And laughter consumes me
with a lightness that feels like floating,

and it is enough.

Sacred Surrender

I listen as my friend recounts, with a softness and delight,
an incident that occurred while hiking
with her friends and their children.

She had fallen and scraped her knee, and there was blood—
enough to warrant some good, old fashioned
comfort and care.

She leaves out the details about the fall itself,
because they aren't important.
It's the next sentence that is the essence of it all:

"And," she shares with a long pause,
"I let them mother me—
I just sat and let the mothers mother me,
with their bandages and ointments,
and I took it all in."

See, as a child, my friend found herself
bathed by her mother in only grit and concrete—
so moments like these contain a powerful medicine.

Her great work in action,
like that of many inner child warriors
who grew up bathed in grit and concrete,
is to surrender to the fact that she, beyond any doubt,
is, and has always been,

worthy of being mothered.

Sacred Language

One favorite part of friendship
with the women in my life,
has been the way that,
all of a sudden,
a turn of phrase,
or mispronounced word,
or highly unusual incident
explained between gasps for air
and bursts of laughter,
is integrated into our sacred language.

The criteria for inclusion
is merely an intuitive knowing
and unconscious commitment
upon hearing it said.

My friend is sharing,
with only admiration,
about the couple
who passed her on a motorcycle—

the back passenger holding tight,
small tennis skirt dancing wildly in the wind,
bright pink thong, free and unapologetically being,
while tanned bum cheeks
soak in the Miami sun.

My friend explained that it was, indeed,
the perfect offset to her minivan-central,
after-school pick-up tornado
of loud children and messy snacks—
the remnants of which
will likely remain for at least another month.

We communicate via video app
and so I see my friend deliver this
message the next morning.
She recalls the juicy juxtaposition
of the motorcycle muse and herself,
and shares, reverently,
that she, too,
would love to feel the wind on her cheeks.

And just like that—
a sacred phrase is born.

Pure Magic

We meet at the park for an hour each day
and we've made this time majestic—
this after-school stretch between
pick up and heading home
to navigate all that accompanies school-age children
and school-age schedules.

We text, "You get the boys, I'll get the lattes?"
We text, "I'm running late, but I have the snacks!"

While the children transmute their energy
in rough and tumble roaring,
we muse over mothering.

She reads our children's star charts
and we make sense of their cosmic beings.

She shuffles oracle cards and
we channel the day's wisdom.

We wonder at the simultaneity
of the contrasting emotions we embody
after giving birth.

Healing our Motherhood wounds together
feels like breathing—
like finally paying tribute to the part of me
I hadn't known was waiting to exhale.

Pure Gold

Friendship amongst women who share
the deep and the dark
and have committed
to carrying each other through it all
is one of life's greatest gifts.

To wake up to a late night text
from a friend
concerned about the resolution
of some major life event
in the life of someone I love,
whom they have never actually met—

is pure gold.

My Best Friend

When we met, her hair fell to her thighs
and she possessed the edgy flare of beyond cool.

When she spoke, she absorbed you with the knowing
that all problems could be solved with love in action.

She unequivocally believed that nature was conspiring
to collaborate with us through our spirals of manifestation.

While the rest of us vied for social acceptance
by not rocking the status quo, she'd redefine it,
laying in a field of flowers,
arms leisurely behind her head,
peering at the clouds, alone,
until one by one we joined,
wanting to feel so powerfully connected
to something beyond ourselves.

To know her was to wonder
if you could take just the smallest essence of her with you—
just a granular piece of her being
to form into a sandy balm and massage into your skin.

If you meet her today, you'll know exactly what I mean.

This Motherhood kaleidoscope has bolded her best hues.

I hope one day you have the chance to meet her.

Happy BIRTHday

We show up to the party, gifts in tow,
ready for whatever concoction of
overstimulation will greet us,
and say, "Happy Birthday," to the wide-eyed,
sugar-induced frenzy of a child.

Knowing too well where I'll find my friend,
I make my way to her familiar kitchen,
I pause her in preparing another tray of snacks,
and hug her, tightly,
repeating the words,
but emphasizing different syllables—
Happy *BIRTH*day.

What I mean is that today,
as I sing to her child,
I celebrate *her*—
her strength,
and the ways in which she broke open
to bring another into form.

A Seasoned Love

My husband and I no longer share poems
that look like sonnets
and sound like yearning.

Our poetry has taken on the form of memes—
the kind that cause eruptive laughter
from the bathroom when one or the other
checks their phone.

These days, we choose our clichés wisely.
Not all anniversaries
are accompanied by flowers
or petals leading to the bedroom,
but there is a moment each day
for dancing in the kitchen,
even amidst arguing—

especially then.

We've discovered an added depth and dimension
that comes with peering, together,
over the edge of annihilation
and still choosing each other.

With young children,
we know we are in the season of "in it",
and that this, too, shall pass,

and we sneak laughter and love
in these tired days,
knowing that if the world should burn
or the oceans crash,
we'll find ourselves hand in hand,
lips fiercely pressed,
ready to emerge on the other side
of whatever comes next.

The Momentary Victor

He walks in the door, gift in hand,
and lets out a deep sigh before saying,
"I forgot to buy the wrapping paper."

As he says it,
he hangs his head low,
but not enough to escape my gaze
and doubly raised eyebrows.

He knows what's coming.

"Oh, don't worry, babe," I say,
a mix of sass and confidence,
as I seductively saunter backward
until my feet meet the stairs.

I hum a bit of "We Are the Champions"
as I turn and climb each step,
victorious fists punching the air,
having just secured one point
in the long-standing marital argument
as to whether or not
the bin of old birthday bags
and used tissue paper
is worth precious real estate
in our small office closet.

Drunk on the Muse

Writing is a curious art.

Some nights, I type furiously
while the children sleep.

I wonder at the pages of poems
that emerged from the depths
of my experience,
my longing,
my surrender.

So moved am I by the way
I've channeled the words
from the universe
of all things beautiful,
that I fall to sleep
excited,
eager, even,
to unwrap them in the morning.

But when we meet again,
they imbue a sense of the unfamiliar,
and taste like sand,

and I wonder how drunk on the muse
I must have been.

Writing Is a Sacred Mother

Writing welcomed me back,
no questions asked,
no apology required,

as though I hadn't abandoned my art,
as though I'd stayed dutifully disciplined,
as though I hadn't wandered
from our sacred space,

as though I hadn't casually placed it in
the back of the refrigerator.

Writing—
wholly, and without reason—

welcomed me back.

The Forces at Play

I sometimes wonder if it's the gravity
of all the roles I've played
or the weight of all the women I've been
that keeps me tethered to the ground.

Fear and Love and Love and Rage

I've mourned the loss of many
ideas and expectations—
none as crushing as that of my
first experience giving birth.

This birth taught me that,
in the introduction to Motherhood,
fear and love are often married,
and I learned that their union following
is nearly impossible to untangle.

For many years, remembering the nothingness
that went according to plan or hope
opened battle wounds I thought had scarred.

I grieved anew every researched idea
I'd attached definition to,
as unnecessary interventions stacked
and removed me from my being.

I'd feel the sting of embarrassment at how
naive I was to have made such plans.

Now, with many moons between us,
when I remember this birth,
I feel like a warrior,
having advocated for
every ounce of agency I could muster
between beeping and breaths.

I can now see artistry
in the scars of this birth story.

I recall my husband's gentle hands,
lightly massaging my back,
and his emotional, "You *are* doing it,"
upon hearing my, "I can't,"

my mother's words calling me back to my truth,
breathing me back to confidence,

the doula's fiendishly clever tactics
to beat the doctor's arbitrary timeline,

my dear friend, divinely on shift at this moment,
laying my son on my chest,

and my father's relief upon seeing me whole.

Now, when I remember this birth,
it's not fear and love,
it's love…

and rage…
at the knowing that there is much work to be done
to prevent the introduction to Motherhood
from being marred with a sense of fear
and a loss of self.

When Boundaries Emerge

Anything done out of obligation is toxic—

words I told my sister in our 20s
and which have me reading poetry
during my rigidly scheduled
school morning prep time.

I'm meant to be packing the lunches,
but I insert some mild rebellion
in this morning's mundane
because it feels oh-so-right,
and I want to.

After 10 minutes of reading,
I return to lunch packing and realize,
I don't want to do this anymore.
And I don't actually have to.

My boundaries surprise me when they emerge.
I don't always anticipate them, and so,
we're not always ready to greet them,

but we've learned that
my feeling static and stuck,
is a sorer fate for all
than my children quickly learning
to pack their own damn lunches.

The Storms Without and Within

There are days without a moment
to hold space for a thought of my own.

Days where the children are insatiable
in their competing calls, needs, and wants
for mama, mama, mama...

These are the days where I find myself frozen,
gazing outward and escaping inward—

feeling myself pause in the eye of the storm,
raging winds wearing my resolve
until I,
too,
rage.

It is also on these days that I now return
more quickly to the intention of myself,
remembering that this storm does not surround me,

but that I AM the storm—

that these raging winds bow to my command—
and so,

I guide myself back to calmer seas.

The Moon and Me

I sometimes wish the Moon's illumination
was without dependence on the positioning
of the Earth and Sun.

I sometimes wish her the freedom
to embody fullness when consumed by creativity,
and to escape in shadow
when needing reflection and restoration.

I sometimes wish her the power
to wax and wane as she chooses—
as it aligns with her deepest desires.

And yet, I wonder if she needs my wishes.

She is, after all, entwined with the cosmos,
anchored in the truth of her celestial core,
always whole—

regardless of my perceptions.

Resentment

She carried me through my season of misalignment.

Sometimes, I miss her dearly.

She never cared where my fingers were pointed,
as long as they were never in my direction.

These days, she is still wild and unruly
and off corroborating someone else's stories.

And I'm just here doing the work—
cleaning mirrors and filing down my nails,
lest I lose an eye.

The Era of Yin

It seems as though every
commercial or podcast
or expert I hear agrees
there is one true solution,
a be-all-end-all solution,
to Motherhood healing.

It's very simple, see
it's all about self-care.

And, when I hear it,
immediate contraction builds
as I'm surrounded by the yang of it all,
and left desperately craving more yin.

Self-care, from what I gather,
is a series of actions,
outward expressions and proof
that we are looking after ourselves—
tending to hair and nails,
exercising, eating well,
and squeezing monthly (or yearly) brunches
into tightly packed schedules
in the sake of saying we put ourselves first.

But I find self-care exhausting.
I tend to run more yang, anyway.

What I want is more of that *soul* care,
that deep in the yin exist and be energy,
that teach me about myself so I am free energy—
more ritual, more listening,
more connecting to the core of me,
more intuitive existing,
more expanding,
more queen and goddess me.

My Mother's Gift

My mother's greatest gift to me is not
the childhood of wonder I experienced,
the sense of adventure she exuded,
the wild laughter she echoed,
or the sage advice she found a way of articulating,
even at her young age.

It is not how she somehow managed to attend
every important school event,
volunteered to lead troops and sports teams,
or how, at 58,
she joined me in my Hypnobirthing classes,
eager to usher in a new narrative of birth.

My mother's greatest gift to me is never once
having claimed a debt for my existence
or making me feel as though my presence
has been any semblance of a burden.

Her greatest gift is pronouncing
in every means of her expression
that she has loved being my mother.

My mother's greatest gift
is the freedom
to fully love myself.

Exhale, and Release

Some days push me to clear all the clutter.

On these particular days,
in part trance and part resolve,
my body enters into contract
with my mind,
and, before I've made the conscious decision,
my running shoes have found their way to my feet
and I recognize the familiar rhythm of a jog.

As my body runs along familiar paths,
my mind races through familiar thoughts,
recycling,
throwing out,
and tidying:

old narratives,
self-imposed expectations,
societal roles,
toxic relationships,
regrets,
comparisons,
fear,
and anything that no longer fits.

I inhale the air of fresh perspectives and possibilities,
and exhale the echoes of all that I cleared,
and I keep breathing,
until I find my way home.

I Am My Most Gracious Host

I have been a myriad of different women,
their ghosts wandering the nooks and crannies
of my psyche, emerging unexpectedly
every now and again.

Some surface dripping with memories,
some prattle on about an unresolved so and so,
others saunter in casually,
donning the denim jacket I wish I'd held onto.

Some run to me,
others gaze stoically, or furiously,
it all depends on the placement of their
eyebrows.

When they find me, I invite them in.
I offer them water, tea, coffee, wine—
whatever they are longing—
they are welcome to.

When they find me,
I tell them it's a dream to see them.

I pull out the old photo albums
and we laugh and cry
and all that comes with nostalgic reunion.

I hug them and tell them they
are welcome to stay as long as they want—
as long as they need.

Nostalgia

In the early years, she visited unannounced.
Her presence evoked a mix of sadness and rage.

Her recalling of the past left me mourning
the fun I used to be and the world I used to roam
and the dreams I wore like tattoos.

With no room available to host such deep-seated
longing and loss, I'd usher her out quickly.
Yet, as the wounds of my Motherhood heal and scar,
I find myself inviting her back in.

When she arrives, I place a chair for her by the fire
and sit on the floor beside her,
fully absorbed as she recounts her version of the past.

Her stories fill me with the hope of a future
filled with adventure reincarnate,
the promise of reawakening, and a grand revival.

This time, when she leaves, I decide to follow her out,
backpack slung over my shoulder—
carrying only the essentials for a wanderlust life
exploring the mountains and rivers of my inner narratives.

I promise we'll meet again on the other side of this present,
soon to be past, where she'll recount,
in all her wisdom,
the strength this moment held.

Aha Moments

I recall yesterday's conversation with my mom
as she and my father drove home
after being out of town for a few weeks.

Because little eager and excited voices
were climbing over mine,
I placed the phone on speaker,
adoring the connection they share
and waiting to hear my children's outpours of
"I missed you" and
"When will we see you?"

Instead, I heard, "Hi Lela,
I love you and don't forget to bring ice cream
when you come over."

I muse to myself about how,
at any given moment,
with no malintent,
children quickly reduce us
to the roles we play for them
or the ways we can better serve them.

She is their grandmother, their abuela, their Lela—
she deserves more than the opportunity to *serve* them.

I make a wish that the next time they're together,
they can truly honor and celebrate *her*,
outside of the roles she plays for them.

This is what I think as my mom,
on her first day back in town,
chauffeurs me to my doctor's appointment
because I've injured my driving foot.

Motherhood Math

The extent to which I return to the
source of myself

is directly proportional to

the extent to which my children
more fully encounter their own.

Too Beautiful to Capture

We share all which words can capture—
the sleepless nights, the messy houses,

the hateful phrases our children uttered flippantly
when the timer went off,
or one had more sprinkles than the other,
or we said, "The street is for walking feet,"
in whatever version of script formula
we've yet again muddled.

We share a language around the tumult
and laugh where others might critique,
because, as often as we can,
we fully embrace what accompanies
raising these beautifully underdeveloped
and erratic beings.

We share what can be expressed,
keeping for ourselves that which transcends
the power of words—
the sacred raw of it all,
which is far better suited for the likes of poetry.

What we will remember, however,
when we linger in rooms
carrying echoes of laughter and play,
will be an essence of a Motherhood
that words could never capture.

Transcendence Is an Altar, Too

Time is a worrisome idol,
stoic to our demands and marching inexorably,
deaf to our pleas for respite—
for even just a moment to profoundly savor
the essence of our children—
to fully explore this cellular love.

Then, without reason,
and in moments
when we beg to arrive
on the other side of a season,
Time, in its own right, remains eternally still.

Why, then, do we worship and contract
within its boundaries?

When will we release our allegiance to Time
and place flowers
at the feet
of a more worthy altar?

Mothering in Community

When we mother in community,
we amplify our magic.

When we open conversation with vulnerability,
offer humor to expose a universal chord
of a mothering experience,
and embrace the emotional hues of
each other's children,

we understand that we are not alone—

and we heal.

I've Got a Mom for That

New mothers—

if you see me at a park,
or store,
or out to dinner,
or jogging,
or anywhere at all—
stop me and speak your pain.

You see, I could write a dissertation
on the nuanced effects of postpartum
on the bodies, minds, and psyches
of all my friends who have given birth,
but I wouldn't draw
from peer-reviewed studies on the matter.

You see, instead of directing you to the literature,
I'm going to direct you to a mama—
a living, breathing mama.
I've got one for every ailment,
and she's waiting for your call.

You're not producing milk? Producing too much?
Your nipples are elastic? Inverted? Different sizes?
You had an episiotomy? C-section?
You think you're getting mastitis?

You're not getting any sleep?
You're wondering which pump? Which stroller?
You've got a prolapsed uterus? You have diastasis recti?
You're waking up drenched in sweat?
I promise, I've got you.

And you see, my mamas won't replace
your doctor or therapist,
but they sure as hell will cradle your pain in their palms
and nurse your soul back to being
because they've been where you are
and made it through whole,
and so will you, mama—

so will you.

Witchy and Wise

When things get itchy, we get witchy.

We light candles,
inhale lavender,
tilt our songs toward the Moon,
and shed our thoughts.

We invite wisdom to pour upon us
and open our hearts to receive.

These rituals seem veiled in mystery
but are our return to a home
of which we were stripped.

We've sought sages on sleep
and repair
and healing—
all to help in this plane of existence.

It's time we seek expansion and consult the oracles of old.

It's time we honor our Motherhood as our mystery school,
embrace this sacred learning as the healing of wounds,
and release the residue of these wounds from our core.

The Collective Wisdom Is Strong

Every mother
holds the weight
of infinite worlds of pain
in her careful palms.

She's learned to craft tools
and carve spaces
for rivers of healing
to run right through
her painful worlds.

Mama, ask her about the weight of her worlds
and the rhythms of her waters.

Ask her how she shapes her tools
so that you, too, can feel your rivers run.

Rhythm and Pulse

The rhythm of our feminine energy
is intuition and emotion,
collaboration and empathy,
and a cyclical nature
of reflection.

The pulse of our masculine energy is
organization and analysis,
linear action and achievement,
advocacy and assertion.

When in sacred union, we are creativity ablaze,
but when they war within, chaos consumes us.

They want to dance.

We must learn to let them.

Reclaiming Our Birthright

Calming our chaos begins
with a solitary step inward—
toward the very essence of our being
to find what has been lost.

If we wander deep enough,
past our fields of expectation,
through our mazes of predetermined plans,
and across our oceans of self-doubt and insecurity,

we'll find Creativity there—

hair loose and loud,
donning paint-splattered overalls,
mystic tea brewing,
waiting patiently for her great conjuring—

waiting for us to summon her forth.

On Preparing for Motherhood

There is no way to plan for Motherhood,
except to bathe in a sea of uncertainty
and hold the truth of yourself
as a life float.

Motherhood is the ultimate act of losing and finding—
and so, if you could plan *her* ahead of time,
the you who would be a mother,
you would never be able to imagine
the depth of being you'd come to know,

because you had not yet lost yourself,

so you could not yet find her.

Because of its complexity,
preparing for Motherhood
has become illogically linked
to preparing for a baby.

Here is how we could prepare for the rebirth of self, instead:

identify how the ways we behave in our relationships
are connected to our childhood wounds,

offer ourselves grace, freely,
when we make mistakes,
or are tired,
or just need it,

learn to fully love ourselves,
shadow side and all,

ask for help when we want it,
not only when it's absolutely necessary,

learn our boundaries and assert them, often,

release expectations of perfection,
in fact, eradicate the very idea from our being,

integrate daily rituals that bring us closer to self—
to sharpen our intuition—
until our knowing cuts through the chaos,

understand that all our reading and research
can never compare to lived experience—
so share less of what we "know" before mothering
and ask already mothers their tools for healing
when hope seems finite,

and mostly,

accept that none of us are *made* for Motherhood,
because Motherhood is making us.

Stepping Into Our Power

It starts with our collective reawakening—
    understanding the ways we've been reduced
    for ease of consumption.

Then, we shed the shackles of definition,
    choosing our *own* words for that which we are
    and all we become throughout our Motherhood.

It continues—

when we stop voicing phrases
    that strip a mother of her knowing,
    implying her pain is not worthy of a space
    as it is not yet significant *enough*—
    changing phrases like,
    "Little kids, little problems,
        or, "Enjoy this time,"
        or, "You'll see,"
        to, "Wow, I remember how hard that was,"

when we remove the word "just" before
    any title we've fought for or found ourselves in,

when we ask each other how we carry
    the weight of our worlds,
    so together, we can engineer
    one better suited for healing.

It's happened when we've removed *ourselves*
   from the ways in which our power is limited,
   and instead, looked to each other
   as the steps and stairways,
   ladders and clouds,
   bridges and rainbows,
   and every practical and mystical
   form we could manifest
   to transcend the limitations of our shadows
   and embrace the fullness of our magic.

Because we ARE the magic.

Acknowledgements

I am profoundly grateful for the women and mothers in my life who have shared the lost and found of this journey. This collection exists because of the village— Michelle B., Lissette H., Judy B., Lily E., Brettlyn W., Simone C., Joanne G., Britta B., Krista H., Alicia H., Krissy T., Praveena S., Mari B., Stephanie D., Milly(not -ie) B., Ana G., Monica O., Ceci C., Bek S., Alexis V., Janeth K., Tammie TM., Erin H., Allison M., Sarah B., Deb F., Jeri W., Cindy P., Lany I., Monica P., Janessa G., Pati L., Julia H., Cat C., and many others.

Jess and Jon Windham, 1/2 SVI, your accountability, belief in, and commitment to this work, along with our shared journey of spirituality and all things "woo" have transformed my expression in this world.

Adri Wilson, Adele Bagley, Audra Obando, and Shana McCann, thank you for not abandoning me despite my pre-children advice, and for continuing to guide me every step of the way.

Katie Willse, you've mothered me in our friendship time and again, showing me endless love and grace, and opening my eyes to the big, wide world. What a gift to do life with you.

Kjersten Faseler and Ellie Beykzadeh, thank you for helping me bring my first artistic expression of Motherhood into form with *Growing our Hearts*. Kjersten, thank you for your constant support in publishing and for your brilliance in editing this book.

Melissa Regina, thank you for your thought partnership throughout the design of this book— you are a truly gifted and wonderful friend.

llse Villamil y Abuela Pepa Jurado, ojalá hubieran podido conocer a los niños. Gracias por tus ejemplos y presencia que aún son palpables en nuestras vidas. Hay cosas que van más allá de las coincidencias.

Betty Piedrahita, gracias por tu cuidado durante el período de postpartum y por abrirle tu corazón y casa a mis hijos.

Tías y primas Jurado, gracias por encarnar el amor que la abuela nos enseñó a compartir tanto en los momentos de felicidad como en los de angustia. Me inspiras todos los días.

Godmother Denise Couture, thank you for celebrating all our special days with a mother's love.

My aunts, Karen and Kitty, thank you endlessly for guiding me back to myself and fostering my journey towards wholeness and healing.

Brigett Potts, thank you for gifting me a book of poems you knew would inspire me to write again and for all the laughter you bring.

Frankie Jurado, our writing and music endeavors have been a dream and have helped me officially claim the title of author— thank you.

Meli Jurado, thank you for taking me with you on the path toward personal and spiritual development, and for pushing me to embrace both my shadow and my magic. And in that light, I also thank Emily Fletcher for her commitment to helping others step into their divinity— the ripples are endless.

My parents, Michele and Frank Jurado, thank you for the sacrifices you made for us, for loving us so fully and deeply, and for the family you built based on laughter, community, and imagination.

My family— I cherish all we've built and continue to build. Writing helped me rediscover parts of me I thought I'd lost, and I thank you for placing it at the center of our family. Javi, this raising young children gig is hard and I'm so proud of all we've done and our commitment to each other. We're a can't-stop-won't-stop kind of vibe and I love you. Cole and Miles, thank you for the love you give so freely everyday and for the way you inspire me to grow and learn.

And to the mysterious force that brings ideas to words and words to form— thank you for choosing me for this book. I am eternally grateful and ready for our next project.

About the Author

Alishea Jurado is an author and educator based in Miami, Florida. With a focus on children's books and Motherhood poems, her work explores the multifaceted roles we play within ourselves, our families, and the communities we call home.

Printed in the USA
CPSIA information can be obtained
at www.ICGtesting.com
CBHW021715170724
11751CB00003B/97